GOAT RECORD KEEPING LOGBOOK

THIS BOOK BELONGS TO:

Name: _____

Phone: _____

Address: _____

Goat Information

Name:	Color:	Sire:
Sex:	Breed:	Dame:
Age:	Registration:	ID Number:
Date of birth:	Identifying marks:	

How Acquired: ☐ Purchased ☐ Born in farm ☐ Leased

Keeping purpose: ☐ Sell ☐ Milk ☐ Meat ☐ Pet ☐ Other

Weight Tracker

Birth	Jan	Feb	Mar	AP	Ma	Jun	Jul	Aug	Sep	Oct	Nov	Dec	**Fin**

Feeding Record

Grain	Jan	Feb	Mar	Ap	May	Jun	Jul	Aug	Sep	Oct	Nov	Dec
Grazing	Jan	Feb	Mar	Ap	May	Jun	Jul	Aug	Sep	Oct	Nov	Dec

Medical Record

Illnesses and Injuries History

Date:	Type of Injury or Illness	Treatment

Vaccination & Supplement History Record

Date	Disease	Supplement used	Result

Testing Record History

Date	Test Performed	Results

Parasite Control Record

Date	Method

Kidding & Breeding Record

Bred to: _____   Date: _____

Kid	Name	Sex	Weight	Markings	Tattoo

Bred to: _____   Date: _____

Kid	Name	Sex	Weight	Markings	Tattoo

Bred to: _____   Date: _____

Kid	Name	Sex	Weight	Markings	Tattoo

Goat Information

Name:	Color:	Sire:
Sex:	Breed:	Dame:
Age:	Registration:	ID Number:
Date of birth:	Identifying marks:	

How Acquired: ☐ Purchased ☐ Born in farm ☐ Leased

Keeping purpose: ☐ Sell ☐ Milk ☐ Meat ☐ Pet ☐ Other

Weight Tracker

Birth	Jan	Feb	Mar	AP	Ma	Jun	Jul	Aug	Sep	Oct	Nov	Dec	**Fin**

Feeding Record

Grain	Jan	Feb	Mar	Ap	May	Jun	Jul	Aug	Sep	Oct	Nov	Dec

Grazing	Jan	Feb	Mar	Ap	May	Jun	Jul	Aug	Sep	Oct	Nov	Dec

Medical Record

Illnesses and Injuries History

Date:	Type of Injury or Illness	Treatment

Vaccination & Supplement History Record

Date	Disease	Supplement used	Result

Testing Record History

Date	Test Performed	Results

Parasite Control Record

Date	Method

Kidding & Breeding Record

Bred to: _____   Date: _____

Kid	Name	Sex	Weight	Markings	Tattoo

Bred to: _____   Date: _____

Kid	Name	Sex	Weight	Markings	Tattoo

Bred to: _____   Date: _____

Kid	Name	Sex	Weight	Markings	Tattoo

Goat Information

Name:	Color:	Sire:
Sex:	Breed:	Dame:
Age:	Registration:	ID Number:
Date of birth:	Identifying marks:	

How Acquired: ☐ Purchased ☐ Born in farm ☐ Leased

Keeping purpose: ☐ Sell ☐ Milk ☐ Meat ☐ Pet ☐ Other

Weight Tracker

Birth	Jan	Feb	Mar	AP	Ma	Jun	Jul	Aug	Sep	Oct	Nov	Dec	**Fin**

Feeding Record

Grain	Jan	Feb	Mar	Ap	May	Jun	Jul	Aug	Sep	Oct	Nov	Dec

Grazing	Jan	Feb	Mar	Ap	May	Jun	Jul	Aug	Sep	Oct	Nov	Dec

Medical Record

Illnesses and Injuries History

Date:	Type of Injury or Illness	Treatment

Vaccination & Supplement History Record

Date	Disease	Supplement used	Result

Testing Record History

Date	Test Performed	Results

Parasite Control Record

Date	Method

Kidding & Breeding Record

Bred to: _____   Date: _____

Kid	Name	Sex	Weight	Markings	Tattoo

Bred to: _____   Date: _____

Kid	Name	Sex	Weight	Markings	Tattoo

Bred to: _____   Date: _____

Kid	Name	Sex	Weight	Markings	Tattoo

Goat Information

Name:	Color:	Sire:
Sex:	Breed:	Dame:
Age:	Registration:	ID Number:
Date of birth:	Identifying marks:	

How Acquired: ☐ Purchased   ☐ Born in farm   ☐ Leased

Keeping purpose: ☐ Sell   ☐ Milk   ☐ Meat   ☐ Pet   ☐ Other

Weight Tracker

Birth	Jan	Feb	Mar	AP	Ma	Jun	Jul	Aug	Sep	Oct	Nov	Dec	**Fin**

Feeding Record

Grain	Jan	Feb	Mar	Ap	May	Jun	Jul	Aug	Sep	Oct	Nov	Dec

Grazing	Jan	Feb	Mar	Ap	May	Jun	Jul	Aug	Sep	Oct	Nov	Dec

Medical Record

Illnesses and Injuries History

Date:	Type of Injury or Illness	Treatment

Vaccination & Supplement History Record

Date	Disease	Supplement used	Result

Testing Record History

Date	Test Performed	Results

Parasite Control Record

Date	Method

Kidding & Breeding Record

Bred to: _____   Date: _____

Kid	Name	Sex	Weight	Markings	Tattoo

Bred to: _____   Date: _____

Kid	Name	Sex	Weight	Markings	Tattoo

Bred to: _____   Date: _____

Kid	Name	Sex	Weight	Markings	Tattoo

Goat Information

Name:	Color:	Sire:
Sex:	Breed:	Dame:
Age:	Registration:	ID Number:
Date of birth:	Identifying marks:	

How Acquired: ☐ Purchased ☐ Born in farm ☐ Leased

Keeping purpose: ☐ Sell ☐ Milk ☐ Meat ☐ Pet ☐ Other

Weight Tracker

Birth	Jan	Feb	Mar	AP	Ma	Jun	Jul	Aug	Sep	Oct	Nov	Dec	Fin

Feeding Record

Grain	Jan	Feb	Mar	Ap	May	Jun	Jul	Aug	Sep	Oct	Nov	Dec

Grazing	Jan	Feb	Mar	Ap	May	Jun	Jul	Aug	Sep	Oct	Nov	Dec

Medical Record

Illnesses and Injuries History

Date:	Type of Injury or Illness	Treatment

Vaccination & Supplement History Record

Date	Disease	Supplement used	Result

Testing Record History

Date	Test Performed	Results

Parasite Control Record

Date	Method

Kidding & Breeding Record

Bred to: _____   Date: _____

Kid	Name	Sex	Weight	Markings	Tattoo

Bred to: _____   Date: _____

Kid	Name	Sex	Weight	Markings	Tattoo

Bred to: _____   Date: _____

Kid	Name	Sex	Weight	Markings	Tattoo

Goat Information

Name:	Color:	Sire:
Sex:	Breed:	Dame:
Age:	Registration:	ID Number:
Date of birth:	Identifying marks:	

How Acquired: ☐ Purchased ☐ Born in farm ☐ Leased

Keeping purpose: ☐ Sell ☐ Milk ☐ Meat ☐ Pet ☐ Other

Weight Tracker

Birth	Jan	Feb	Mar	AP	Ma	Jun	Jul	Aug	Sep	Oct	Nov	Dec	**Fin**

Feeding Record

Grain	Jan	Feb	Mar	Ap	May	Jun	Jul	Aug	Sep	Oct	Nov	Dec

Grazing	Jan	Feb	Mar	Ap	May	Jun	Jul	Aug	Sep	Oct	Nov	Dec

Medical Record

Illnesses and Injuries History

Date:	Type of Injury or Illness	Treatment

Vaccination & Supplement History Record

Date	Disease	Supplement used	Result

Testing Record History

Date	Test Performed	Results

Parasite Control Record

Date	Method

Kidding & Breeding Record

Bred to: _____   Date: _____

Kid	Name	Sex	Weight	Markings	Tattoo

Bred to: _____   Date: _____

Kid	Name	Sex	Weight	Markings	Tattoo

Bred to: _____   Date: _____

Kid	Name	Sex	Weight	Markings	Tattoo

Goat Information

Name:	Color:	Sire:
Sex:	Breed:	Dame:
Age:	Registration:	ID Number:
Date of birth:	Identifying marks:	

How Acquired: ☐ Purchased   ☐ Born in farm   ☐ Leased

Keeping purpose: ☐ Sell   ☐ Milk   ☐ Meat   ☐ Pet   ☐ Other

Weight Tracker

Birth	Jan	Feb	Mar	AP	Ma	Jun	Jul	Aug	Sep	Oct	Nov	Dec	**Fin**

Feeding Record

Grain	Jan	Feb	Mar	Ap	May	Jun	Jul	Aug	Sep	Oct	Nov	Dec

Grazing	Jan	Feb	Mar	Ap	May	Jun	Jul	Aug	Sep	Oct	Nov	Dec

Medical Record

Illnesses and Injuries History

Date:	Type of Injury or Illness	Treatment

Vaccination & Supplement History Record

Date	Disease	Supplement used	Result

Testing Record History

Date	Test Performed	Results

Parasite Control Record

Date	Method

Kidding & Breeding Record

Bred to: _____ Date: _____

Kid	Name	Sex	Weight	Markings	Tattoo

Bred to: _____ Date: _____

Kid	Name	Sex	Weight	Markings	Tattoo

Bred to: _____ Date: _____

Kid	Name	Sex	Weight	Markings	Tattoo

Goat Information

Name:	Color:	Sire:
Sex:	Breed:	Dame:
Age:	Registration:	ID Number:
Date of birth:	Identifying marks:	

How Acquired: ☐ Purchased   ☐ Born in farm   ☐ Leased

Keeping purpose: ☐ Sell   ☐ Milk   ☐ Meat   ☐ Pet   ☐ Other

Weight Tracker

Birth	Jan	Feb	Mar	AP	Ma	Jun	Jul	Aug	Sep	Oct	Nov	Dec	**Fin**

Feeding Record

Grain	Jan	Feb	Mar	Ap	May	Jun	Jul	Aug	Sep	Oct	Nov	Dec

Grazing	Jan	Feb	Mar	Ap	May	Jun	Jul	Aug	Sep	Oct	Nov	Dec

Medical Record

Illnesses and Injuries History

Date:	Type of Injury or Illness	Treatment

Vaccination & Supplement History Record

Date	Disease	Supplement used	Result

Testing Record History

Date	Test Performed	Results

Parasite Control Record

Date	Method

Kidding & Breeding Record

Bred to: _____ Date: _____

Kid	Name	Sex	Weight	Markings	Tattoo

Bred to: _____ Date: _____

Kid	Name	Sex	Weight	Markings	Tattoo

Bred to: _____ Date: _____

Kid	Name	Sex	Weight	Markings	Tattoo

Goat Information

Name:	Color:	Sire:
Sex:	Breed:	Dame:
Age:	Registration:	ID Number:
Date of birth:	Identifying marks:	

How Acquired: ☐ Purchased   ☐ Born in farm   ☐ Leased

Keeping purpose: ☐ Sell   ☐ Milk   ☐ Meat   ☐ Pet   ☐ Other

Weight Tracker

Birth	Jan	Feb	Mar	AP	Ma	Jun	Jul	Aug	Sep	Oct	Nov	Dec	Fin

Feeding Record

Grain	Jan	Feb	Mar	Ap	May	Jun	Jul	Aug	Sep	Oct	Nov	Dec
Grazing	Jan	Feb	Mar	Ap	May	Jun	Jul	Aug	Sep	Oct	Nov	Dec

Medical Record

Illnesses and Injuries History

Date:	Type of Injury or Illness	Treatment

Vaccination & Supplement History Record

Date	Disease	Supplement used	Result

Testing Record History

Date	Test Performed	Results

Parasite Control Record

Date	Method

Kidding & Breeding Record

Bred to: _____   Date: _____

Kid	Name	Sex	Weight	Markings	Tattoo

Bred to: _____   Date: _____

Kid	Name	Sex	Weight	Markings	Tattoo

Bred to: _____   Date: _____

Kid	Name	Sex	Weight	Markings	Tattoo

Goat Information

Name:	Color:	Sire:
Sex:	Breed:	Dame:
Age:	Registration:	ID Number:
Date of birth:	Identifying marks:	

How Acquired: ☐ Purchased   ☐ Born in farm   ☐ Leased

Keeping purpose: ☐ Sell   ☐ Milk   ☐ Meat   ☐ Pet   ☐ Other

Weight Tracker

Birth	Jan	Feb	Mar	AP	Ma	Jun	Jul	Aug	Sep	Oct	Nov	Dec	Fin

Feeding Record

Grain	Jan	Feb	Mar	Ap	May	Jun	Jul	Aug	Sep	Oct	Nov	Dec

Grazing	Jan	Feb	Mar	Ap	May	Jun	Jul	Aug	Sep	Oct	Nov	Dec

Medical Record

Illnesses and Injuries History

Date:	Type of Injury or Illness	Treatment

Vaccination & Supplement History Record

Date	Disease	Supplement used	Result

Testing Record History

Date	Test Performed	Results

Parasite Control Record

Date	Method

Kidding & Breeding Record

Bred to: _____   Date: _____

Kid	Name	Sex	Weight	Markings	Tattoo

Bred to: _____   Date: _____

Kid	Name	Sex	Weight	Markings	Tattoo

Bred to: _____   Date: _____

Kid	Name	Sex	Weight	Markings	Tattoo

Goat Information

Name:	Color:	Sire:
Sex:	Breed:	Dame:
Age:	Registration:	ID Number:
Date of birth:	Identifying marks:	

How Acquired: ☐ Purchased ☐ Born in farm ☐ Leased

Keeping purpose: ☐ Sell ☐ Milk ☐ Meat ☐ Pet ☐ Other

Weight Tracker

Birth	Jan	Feb	Mar	AP	Ma	Jun	Jul	Aug	Sep	Oct	Nov	Dec	Fin

Feeding Record

Grain	Jan	Feb	Mar	Ap	May	Jun	Jul	Aug	Sep	Oct	Nov	Dec
Grazing	Jan	Feb	Mar	Ap	May	Jun	Jul	Aug	Sep	Oct	Nov	Dec

Medical Record

Illnesses and Injuries History

Date:	Type of Injury or Illness	Treatment

Vaccination & Supplement History Record

Date	Disease	Supplement used	Result

Testing Record History

Date	Test Performed	Results

Parasite Control Record

Date	Method

Kidding & Breeding Record

Bred to: _____   Date: _____

Kid	Name	Sex	Weight	Markings	Tattoo

Bred to: _____   Date: _____

Kid	Name	Sex	Weight	Markings	Tattoo

Bred to: _____   Date: _____

Kid	Name	Sex	Weight	Markings	Tattoo

Goat Information

Name:	Color:	Sire:
Sex:	Breed:	Dame:
Age:	Registration:	ID Number:
Date of birth:	Identifying marks:	

How Acquired: ☐ Purchased ☐ Born in farm ☐ Leased

Keeping purpose: ☐ Sell ☐ Milk ☐ Meat ☐ Pet ☐ Other

Weight Tracker

Birth	Jan	Feb	Mar	AP	Ma	Jun	Jul	Aug	Sep	Oct	Nov	Dec	**Fin**

Feeding Record

Grain	Jan	Feb	Mar	Ap	May	Jun	Jul	Aug	Sep	Oct	Nov	Dec

Grazing	Jan	Feb	Mar	Ap	May	Jun	Jul	Aug	Sep	Oct	Nov	Dec

Medical Record

Illnesses and Injuries History

Date:	Type of Injury or Illness	Treatment

Vaccination & Supplement History Record

Date	Disease	Supplement used	Result

Testing Record History

Date	Test Performed	Results

Parasite Control Record

Date	Method

Kidding & Breeding Record

Bred to: _____   Date: _____

Kid	Name	Sex	Weight	Markings	Tattoo

Bred to: _____   Date: _____

Kid	Name	Sex	Weight	Markings	Tattoo

Bred to: _____   Date: _____

Kid	Name	Sex	Weight	Markings	Tattoo

Goat Information

Name:	Color:	Sire:
Sex:	Breed:	Dame:
Age:	Registration:	ID Number:
Date of birth:	Identifying marks:	

How Acquired: ☐ Purchased ☐ Born in farm ☐ Leased

Keeping purpose: ☐ Sell ☐ Milk ☐ Meat ☐ Pet ☐ Other

Weight Tracker

Birth	Jan	Feb	Mar	AP	Ma	Jun	Jul	Aug	Sep	Oct	Nov	Dec	**Fin**

Feeding Record

Grain	Jan	Feb	Mar	Ap	May	Jun	Jul	Aug	Sep	Oct	Nov	Dec
Grazing	Jan	Feb	Mar	Ap	May	Jun	Jul	Aug	Sep	Oct	Nov	Dec

Medical Record

Illnesses and Injuries History

Date:	Type of Injury or Illness	Treatment

Vaccination & Supplement History Record

Date	Disease	Supplement used	Result

Testing Record History

Date	Test Performed	Results

Parasite Control Record

Date	Method

Kidding & Breeding Record

Bred to: _____   Date: _____

Kid	Name	Sex	Weight	Markings	Tattoo

Bred to: _____   Date: _____

Kid	Name	Sex	Weight	Markings	Tattoo

Bred to: _____   Date: _____

Kid	Name	Sex	Weight	Markings	Tattoo

Goat Information

Name:	Color:	Sire:
Sex:	Breed:	Dame:
Age:	Registration:	ID Number:
Date of birth:	Identifying marks:	

How Acquired: ☐ Purchased ☐ Born in farm ☐ Leased

Keeping purpose: ☐ Sell ☐ Milk ☐ Meat ☐ Pet ☐ Other

Weight Tracker

Birth	Jan	Feb	Mar	AP	Ma	Jun	Jul	Aug	Sep	Oct	Nov	Dec	**Fin**

Feeding Record

Grain	Jan	Feb	Mar	Ap	May	Jun	Jul	Aug	Sep	Oct	Nov	Dec

Grazing	Jan	Feb	Mar	Ap	May	Jun	Jul	Aug	Sep	Oct	Nov	Dec

Medical Record

Illnesses and Injuries History

Date:	Type of Injury or Illness	Treatment

Vaccination & Supplement History Record

Date	Disease	Supplement used	Result

Testing Record History

Date	Test Performed	Results

Parasite Control Record

Date	Method

Kidding & Breeding Record

Bred to: _____ **Date:** _____

Kid	Name	Sex	Weight	Markings	Tattoo

Bred to: _____ **Date:** _____

Kid	Name	Sex	Weight	Markings	Tattoo

Bred to: _____ **Date:** _____

Kid	Name	Sex	Weight	Markings	Tattoo

Goat Information

Name:	Color:	Sire:
Sex:	Breed:	Dame:
Age:	Registration:	ID Number:
Date of birth:	Identifying marks:	

How Acquired: ☐ Purchased ☐ Born in farm ☐ Leased

Keeping purpose: ☐ Sell ☐ Milk ☐ Meat ☐ Pet ☐ Other

Weight Tracker

Birth	Jan	Feb	Mar	AP	Ma	Jun	Jul	Aug	Sep	Oct	Nov	Dec	Fin

Feeding Record

Grain	Jan	Feb	Mar	Ap	May	Jun	Jul	Aug	Sep	Oct	Nov	Dec
Grazing	Jan	Feb	Mar	Ap	May	Jun	Jul	Aug	Sep	Oct	Nov	Dec

Medical Record

Illnesses and Injuries History

Date:	Type of Injury or Illness	Treatment

Vaccination & Supplement History Record

Date	Disease	Supplement used	Result

Testing Record History

Date	Test Performed	Results

Parasite Control Record

Date	Method

Kidding & Breeding Record

Bred to: _____   Date: _____

Kid	Name	Sex	Weight	Markings	Tattoo

Bred to: _____   Date: _____

Kid	Name	Sex	Weight	Markings	Tattoo

Bred to: _____   Date: _____

Kid	Name	Sex	Weight	Markings	Tattoo

Goat Information

Name:	Color:	Sire:
Sex:	Breed:	Dame:
Age:	Registration:	ID Number:
Date of birth:	Identifying marks:	

How Acquired: ☐ Purchased   ☐ Born in farm   ☐ Leased

Keeping purpose: ☐ Sell   ☐ Milk   ☐ Meat   ☐ Pet   ☐ Other

Weight Tracker

Birth	Jan	Feb	Mar	AP	Ma	Jun	Jul	Aug	Sep	Oct	Nov	Dec	**Fin**

Feeding Record

Grain	Jan	Feb	Mar	Ap	May	Jun	Jul	Aug	Sep	Oct	Nov	Dec

Grazing	Jan	Feb	Mar	Ap	May	Jun	Jul	Aug	Sep	Oct	Nov	Dec

Medical Record

Illnesses and Injuries History

Date:	Type of Injury or Illness	Treatment

Vaccination & Supplement History Record

Date	Disease	Supplement used	Result

Testing Record History

Date	Test Performed	Results

Parasite Control Record

Date	Method

Kidding & Breeding Record

Bred to: _____   Date: _____

Kid	Name	Sex	Weight	Markings	Tattoo

Bred to: _____   Date: _____

Kid	Name	Sex	Weight	Markings	Tattoo

Bred to: _____   Date: _____

Kid	Name	Sex	Weight	Markings	Tattoo

Goat Information

Name:	Color:	Sire:
Sex:	Breed:	Dame:
Age:	Registration:	ID Number:
Date of birth:	Identifying marks:	

How Acquired: ☐ Purchased ☐ Born in farm ☐ Leased

Keeping purpose: ☐ Sell ☐ Milk ☐ Meat ☐ Pet ☐ Other

Weight Tracker

Birth	Jan	Feb	Mar	AP	Ma	Jun	Jul	Aug	Sep	Oct	Nov	Dec	**Fin**

Feeding Record

Grain	Jan	Feb	Mar	Ap	May	Jun	Jul	Aug	Sep	Oct	Nov	Dec

Grazing	Jan	Feb	Mar	Ap	May	Jun	Jul	Aug	Sep	Oct	Nov	Dec

Medical Record

Illnesses and Injuries History

Date:	Type of Injury or Illness	Treatment

Vaccination & Supplement History Record

Date	Disease	Supplement used	Result

Testing Record History

Date	Test Performed	Results

Parasite Control Record

Date	Method

Kidding & Breeding Record

Bred to: _____   Date: _____

Kid	Name	Sex	Weight	Markings	Tattoo

Bred to: _____   Date: _____

Kid	Name	Sex	Weight	Markings	Tattoo

Bred to: _____   Date: _____

Kid	Name	Sex	Weight	Markings	Tattoo

Goat Information

Name:	Color:	Sire:
Sex:	Breed:	Dame:
Age:	Registration:	ID Number:
Date of birth:	Identifying marks:	

How Acquired: ☐ Purchased ☐ Born in farm ☐ Leased

Keeping purpose: ☐ Sell ☐ Milk ☐ Meat ☐ Pet ☐ Other

Weight Tracker

Birth	Jan	Feb	Mar	AP	Ma	Jun	Jul	Aug	Sep	Oct	Nov	Dec	**Fin**

Feeding Record

Grain	Jan	Feb	Mar	Ap	May	Jun	Jul	Aug	Sep	Oct	Nov	Dec

Grazing	Jan	Feb	Mar	Ap	May	Jun	Jul	Aug	Sep	Oct	Nov	Dec

Medical Record

Illnesses and Injuries History

Date:	Type of Injury or Illness	Treatment

Vaccination & Supplement History Record

Date	Disease	Supplement used	Result

Testing Record History

Date	Test Performed	Results

Parasite Control Record

Date	Method

Kidding & Breeding Record

Bred to: _____   Date: _____

Kid	Name	Sex	Weight	Markings	Tattoo

Bred to: _____   Date: _____

Kid	Name	Sex	Weight	Markings	Tattoo

Bred to: _____   Date: _____

Kid	Name	Sex	Weight	Markings	Tattoo

Goat Information

Name:	Color:	Sire:
Sex:	Breed:	Dame:
Age:	Registration:	ID Number:
Date of birth:	Identifying marks:	

How Acquired: ☐ Purchased ☐ Born in farm ☐ Leased

Keeping purpose: ☐ Sell ☐ Milk ☐ Meat ☐ Pet ☐ Other

Weight Tracker

Birth	Jan	Feb	Mar	AP	Ma	Jun	Jul	Aug	Sep	Oct	Nov	Dec	Fin

Feeding Record

Grain	Jan	Feb	Mar	Ap	May	Jun	Jul	Aug	Sep	Oct	Nov	Dec

Grazing	Jan	Feb	Mar	Ap	May	Jun	Jul	Aug	Sep	Oct	Nov	Dec

Medical Record

Illnesses and Injuries History

Date:	Type of Injury or Illness	Treatment

Vaccination & Supplement History Record

Date	Disease	Supplement used	Result

Testing Record History

Date	Test Performed	Results

Parasite Control Record

Date	Method

Kidding & Breeding Record

Bred to: _____ Date: _____

Kid	Name	Sex	Weight	Markings	Tattoo

Bred to: _____ Date: _____

Kid	Name	Sex	Weight	Markings	Tattoo

Bred to: _____ Date: _____

Kid	Name	Sex	Weight	Markings	Tattoo

Goat Information

Name:	Color:	Sire:
Sex:	Breed:	Dame:
Age:	Registration:	ID Number:
Date of birth:	Identifying marks:	

How Acquired: ☐ Purchased ☐ Born in farm ☐ Leased

Keeping purpose: ☐ Sell ☐ Milk ☐ Meat ☐ Pet ☐ Other

Weight Tracker

Birth	Jan	Feb	Mar	AP	Ma	Jun	Jul	Aug	Sep	Oct	Nov	Dec	**Fin**

Feeding Record

Grain	Jan	Feb	Mar	Ap	May	Jun	Jul	Aug	Sep	Oct	Nov	Dec
Grazing	Jan	Feb	Mar	Ap	May	Jun	Jul	Aug	Sep	Oct	Nov	Dec

Medical Record

Illnesses and Injuries History

Date:	Type of Injury or Illness	Treatment

Vaccination & Supplement History Record

Date	Disease	Supplement used	Result

Testing Record History

Date	Test Performed	Results

Parasite Control Record

Date	Method

Kidding & Breeding Record

Bred to: _____   Date: _____

Kid	Name	Sex	Weight	Markings	Tattoo

Bred to: _____   Date: _____

Kid	Name	Sex	Weight	Markings	Tattoo

Bred to: _____   Date: _____

Kid	Name	Sex	Weight	Markings	Tattoo

Goat Information

Name:	Color:	Sire:
Sex:	Breed:	Dame:
Age:	Registration:	ID Number:
Date of birth:	Identifying marks:	

How Acquired: ☐ Purchased ☐ Born in farm ☐ Leased

Keeping purpose: ☐ Sell ☐ Milk ☐ Meat ☐ Pet ☐ Other

Weight Tracker

Birth	Jan	Feb	Mar	AP	Ma	Jun	Jul	Aug	Sep	Oct	Nov	Dec	**Fin**

Feeding Record

Grain	Jan	Feb	Mar	Ap	May	Jun	Jul	Aug	Sep	Oct	Nov	Dec
Grazing	Jan	Feb	Mar	Ap	May	Jun	Jul	Aug	Sep	Oct	Nov	Dec

Medical Record

Illnesses and Injuries History

Date:	Type of Injury or Illness	Treatment

Vaccination & Supplement History Record

Date	Disease	Supplement used	Result

Testing Record History

Date	Test Performed	Results

Parasite Control Record

Date	Method

Kidding & Breeding Record

Bred to: _____   Date: _____

Kid	Name	Sex	Weight	Markings	Tattoo

Bred to: _____   Date: _____

Kid	Name	Sex	Weight	Markings	Tattoo

Bred to: _____   Date: _____

Kid	Name	Sex	Weight	Markings	Tattoo

Goat Information

Name:	Color:	Sire:
Sex:	Breed:	Dame:
Age:	Registration:	ID Number:
Date of birth:	Identifying marks:	

How Acquired: ☐ Purchased   ☐ Born in farm   ☐ Leased

Keeping purpose: ☐ Sell   ☐ Milk   ☐ Meat   ☐ Pet   ☐ Other

Weight Tracker

Birth	Jan	Feb	Mar	AP	Ma	Jun	Jul	Aug	Sep	Oct	Nov	Dec	**Fin**

Feeding Record

Grain	Jan	Feb	Mar	Ap	May	Jun	Jul	Aug	Sep	Oct	Nov	Dec

Grazing	Jan	Feb	Mar	Ap	May	Jun	Jul	Aug	Sep	Oct	Nov	Dec

Medical Record

Illnesses and Injuries History

Date:	Type of Injury or Illness	Treatment

Vaccination & Supplement History Record

Date	Disease	Supplement used	Result

Testing Record History

Date	Test Performed	Results

Parasite Control Record

Date	Method

Kidding & Breeding Record

Bred to: _____   Date: _____

Kid	Name	Sex	Weight	Markings	Tattoo

Bred to: _____   Date: _____

Kid	Name	Sex	Weight	Markings	Tattoo

Bred to: _____   Date: _____

Kid	Name	Sex	Weight	Markings	Tattoo

Goat Information

Name:	Color:	Sire:
Sex:	Breed:	Dame:
Age:	Registration:	ID Number:
Date of birth:	Identifying marks:	

How Acquired: ☐ Purchased ☐ Born in farm ☐ Leased

Keeping purpose: ☐ Sell ☐ Milk ☐ Meat ☐ Pet ☐ Other

Weight Tracker

Birth	Jan	Feb	Mar	AP	Ma	Jun	Jul	Aug	Sep	Oct	Nov	Dec	**Fin**

Feeding Record

Grain	Jan	Feb	Mar	Ap	May	Jun	Jul	Aug	Sep	Oct	Nov	Dec

Grazing	Jan	Feb	Mar	Ap	May	Jun	Jul	Aug	Sep	Oct	Nov	Dec

Medical Record

Illnesses and Injuries History

Date:	Type of Injury or Illness	Treatment

Vaccination & Supplement History Record

Date	Disease	Supplement used	Result

Testing Record History

Date	Test Performed	Results

Parasite Control Record

Date	Method

Kidding & Breeding Record

Bred to: _____   **Date:** _____

Kid	Name	Sex	Weight	Markings	Tattoo

Bred to: _____   **Date:** _____

Kid	Name	Sex	Weight	Markings	Tattoo

Bred to: _____   **Date:** _____

Kid	Name	Sex	Weight	Markings	Tattoo

Goat Information

Name:	Color:	Sire:
Sex:	Breed:	Dame:
Age:	Registration:	ID Number:
Date of birth:	Identifying marks:	

How Acquired: ☐ Purchased ☐ Born in farm ☐ Leased

Keeping purpose: ☐ Sell ☐ Milk ☐ Meat ☐ Pet ☐ Other

Weight Tracker

Birth	Jan	Feb	Mar	AP	Ma	Jun	Jul	Aug	Sep	Oct	Nov	Dec	Fin

Feeding Record

Grain	Jan	Feb	Mar	Ap	May	Jun	Jul	Aug	Sep	Oct	Nov	Dec

Grazing	Jan	Feb	Mar	Ap	May	Jun	Jul	Aug	Sep	Oct	Nov	Dec

Medical Record

Illnesses and Injuries History

Date:	Type of Injury or Illness	Treatment

Vaccination & Supplement History Record

Date	Disease	Supplement used	Result

Testing Record History

Date	Test Performed	Results

Parasite Control Record

Date	Method

Kidding & Breeding Record

Bred to: _____ Date: _____

Kid	Name	Sex	Weight	Markings	Tattoo

Bred to: _____ Date: _____

Kid	Name	Sex	Weight	Markings	Tattoo

Bred to: _____ Date: _____

Kid	Name	Sex	Weight	Markings	Tattoo

Goat Information

Name:	Color:	Sire:
Sex:	Breed:	Dame:
Age:	Registration:	ID Number:
Date of birth:	Identifying marks:	

How Acquired: ☐ Purchased ☐ Born in farm ☐ Leased

Keeping purpose: ☐ Sell ☐ Milk ☐ Meat ☐ Pet ☐ Other

Weight Tracker

Birth	Jan	Feb	Mar	AP	Ma	Jun	Jul	Aug	Sep	Oct	Nov	Dec	Fin

Feeding Record

Grain	Jan	Feb	Mar	Ap	May	Jun	Jul	Aug	Sep	Oct	Nov	Dec
Grazing	Jan	Feb	Mar	Ap	May	Jun	Jul	Aug	Sep	Oct	Nov	Dec

Medical Record

Illnesses and Injuries History

Date:	Type of Injury or Illness	Treatment

Vaccination & Supplement History Record

Date	Disease	Supplement used	Result

Testing Record History

Date	Test Performed	Results

Parasite Control Record

Date	Method

Kidding & Breeding Record

Bred to: _____   Date: _____

Kid	Name	Sex	Weight	Markings	Tattoo

Bred to: _____   Date: _____

Kid	Name	Sex	Weight	Markings	Tattoo

Bred to: _____   Date: _____

Kid	Name	Sex	Weight	Markings	Tattoo

Goat Information

Name:	Color:	Sire:
Sex:	Breed:	Dame:
Age:	Registration:	ID Number:
Date of birth:	Identifying marks:	

How Acquired: ☐ Purchased ☐ Born in farm ☐ Leased

Keeping purpose: ☐ Sell ☐ Milk ☐ Meat ☐ Pet ☐ Other

Weight Tracker

Birth	Jan	Feb	Mar	AP	Ma	Jun	Jul	Aug	Sep	Oct	Nov	Dec	Fin

Feeding Record

Grain	Jan	Feb	Mar	Ap	May	Jun	Jul	Aug	Sep	Oct	Nov	Dec

Grazing	Jan	Feb	Mar	Ap	May	Jun	Jul	Aug	Sep	Oct	Nov	Dec

Medical Record

Illnesses and Injuries History

Date:	Type of Injury or Illness	Treatment

Vaccination & Supplement History Record

Date	Disease	Supplement used	Result

Testing Record History

Date	Test Performed	Results

Parasite Control Record

Date	Method

Kidding & Breeding Record

Bred to: _____ Date: _____

Kid	Name	Sex	Weight	Markings	Tattoo

Bred to: _____ Date: _____

Kid	Name	Sex	Weight	Markings	Tattoo

Bred to: _____ Date: _____

Kid	Name	Sex	Weight	Markings	Tattoo

Goat Information

Name:	Color:	Sire:
Sex:	Breed:	Dame:
Age:	Registration:	ID Number:
Date of birth:	Identifying marks:	

How Acquired: ☐ Purchased ☐ Born in farm ☐ Leased

Keeping purpose: ☐ Sell ☐ Milk ☐ Meat ☐ Pet ☐ Other

Weight Tracker

Birth	Jan	Feb	Mar	AP	Ma	Jun	Jul	Aug	Sep	Oct	Nov	Dec	Fin

Feeding Record

Grain	Jan	Feb	Mar	Ap	May	Jun	Jul	Aug	Sep	Oct	Nov	Dec

Grazing	Jan	Feb	Mar	Ap	May	Jun	Jul	Aug	Sep	Oct	Nov	Dec

Medical Record

Illnesses and Injuries History

Date:	Type of Injury or Illness	Treatment

Vaccination & Supplement History Record

Date	Disease	Supplement used	Result

Testing Record History

Date	Test Performed	Results

Parasite Control Record

Date	Method

Kidding & Breeding Record

Bred to: _____   Date: _____

Kid	Name	Sex	Weight	Markings	Tattoo

Bred to: _____   Date: _____

Kid	Name	Sex	Weight	Markings	Tattoo

Bred to: _____   Date: _____

Kid	Name	Sex	Weight	Markings	Tattoo

Goat Information

Name:	Color:	Sire:
Sex:	Breed:	Dame:
Age:	Registration:	ID Number:
Date of birth:	Identifying marks:	

How Acquired: ☐ Purchased ☐ Born in farm ☐ Leased

Keeping purpose: ☐ Sell ☐ Milk ☐ Meat ☐ Pet ☐ Other

Weight Tracker

Birth	Jan	Feb	Mar	AP	Ma	Jun	Jul	Aug	Sep	Oct	Nov	Dec	**Fin**

Feeding Record

Grain	Jan	Feb	Mar	Ap	May	Jun	Jul	Aug	Sep	Oct	Nov	Dec

Grazing	Jan	Feb	Mar	Ap	May	Jun	Jul	Aug	Sep	Oct	Nov	Dec

Medical Record

Illnesses and Injuries History

Date:	Type of Injury or Illness	Treatment

Vaccination & Supplement History Record

Date	Disease	Supplement used	Result

Testing Record History

Date	Test Performed	Results

Parasite Control Record

Date	Method

Kidding & Breeding Record

Bred to: _____   Date: _____

Kid	Name	Sex	Weight	Markings	Tattoo

Bred to: _____   Date: _____

Kid	Name	Sex	Weight	Markings	Tattoo

Bred to: _____   Date: _____

Kid	Name	Sex	Weight	Markings	Tattoo

Goat Information

Name:	Color:	Sire:
Sex:	Breed:	Dame:
Age:	Registration:	ID Number:
Date of birth:	Identifying marks:	

How Acquired: ☐ Purchased   ☐ Born in farm   ☐ Leased

Keeping purpose: ☐ Sell   ☐ Milk   ☐ Meat   ☐ Pet   ☐ Other

Weight Tracker

Birth	Jan	Feb	Mar	AP	Ma	Jun	Jul	Aug	Sep	Oct	Nov	Dec	Fin

Feeding Record

Grain	Jan	Feb	Mar	Ap	May	Jun	Jul	Aug	Sep	Oct	Nov	Dec
Grazing	Jan	Feb	Mar	Ap	May	Jun	Jul	Aug	Sep	Oct	Nov	Dec

Medical Record

Illnesses and Injuries History

Date:	Type of Injury or Illness	Treatment

Vaccination & Supplement History Record

Date	Disease	Supplement used	Result

Testing Record History

Date	Test Performed	Results

Parasite Control Record

Date	Method

Kidding & Breeding Record

Bred to: _____   Date: _____

Kid	Name	Sex	Weight	Markings	Tattoo

Bred to: _____   Date: _____

Kid	Name	Sex	Weight	Markings	Tattoo

Bred to: _____   Date: _____

Kid	Name	Sex	Weight	Markings	Tattoo

Goat Information

Name:	Color:	Sire:
Sex:	Breed:	Dame:
Age:	Registration:	ID Number:
Date of birth:	Identifying marks:	

How Acquired: ☐ Purchased ☐ Born in farm ☐ Leased

Keeping purpose: ☐ Sell ☐ Milk ☐ Meat ☐ Pet ☐ Other

Weight Tracker

Birth	Jan	Feb	Mar	AP	Ma	Jun	Jul	Aug	Sep	Oct	Nov	Dec	**Fin**

Feeding Record

Grain	Jan	Feb	Mar	Ap	May	Jun	Jul	Aug	Sep	Oct	Nov	Dec

Grazing	Jan	Feb	Mar	Ap	May	Jun	Jul	Aug	Sep	Oct	Nov	Dec

Medical Record

Illnesses and Injuries History

Date:	Type of Injury or Illness	Treatment

Vaccination & Supplement History Record

Date	Disease	Supplement used	Result

Testing Record History

Date	Test Performed	Results

Parasite Control Record

Date	Method

Kidding & Breeding Record

Bred to: _____   Date: _____

Kid	Name	Sex	Weight	Markings	Tattoo

Bred to: _____   Date: _____

Kid	Name	Sex	Weight	Markings	Tattoo

Bred to: _____   Date: _____

Kid	Name	Sex	Weight	Markings	Tattoo

Goat Information

Name:	Color:	Sire:
Sex:	Breed:	Dame:
Age:	Registration:	ID Number:
Date of birth:	Identifying marks:	

How Acquired: ☐ Purchased ☐ Born in farm ☐ Leased

Keeping purpose: ☐ Sell ☐ Milk ☐ Meat ☐ Pet ☐ Other

Weight Tracker

Birth	Jan	Feb	Mar	AP	Ma	Jun	Jul	Aug	Sep	Oct	Nov	Dec	Fin

Feeding Record

Grain	Jan	Feb	Mar	Ap	May	Jun	Jul	Aug	Sep	Oct	Nov	Dec
Grazing	Jan	Feb	Mar	Ap	May	Jun	Jul	Aug	Sep	Oct	Nov	Dec

Medical Record

Illnesses and Injuries History

Date:	Type of Injury or Illness	Treatment

Vaccination & Supplement History Record

Date	Disease	Supplement used	Result

Testing Record History

Date	Test Performed	Results

Parasite Control Record

Date	Method

Kidding & Breeding Record

Bred to: _____   Date: _____

Kid	Name	Sex	Weight	Markings	Tattoo

Bred to: _____   Date: _____

Kid	Name	Sex	Weight	Markings	Tattoo

Bred to: _____   Date: _____

Kid	Name	Sex	Weight	Markings	Tattoo

Goat Information

Name:	Color:	Sire:
Sex:	Breed:	Dame:
Age:	Registration:	ID Number:
Date of birth:	Identifying marks:	

How Acquired: ☐ Purchased ☐ Born in farm ☐ Leased

Keeping purpose: ☐ Sell ☐ Milk ☐ Meat ☐ Pet ☐ Other

Weight Tracker

Birth	Jan	Feb	Mar	AP	Ma	Jun	Jul	Aug	Sep	Oct	Nov	Dec	**Fin**

Feeding Record

Grain	Jan	Feb	Mar	Ap	May	Jun	Jul	Aug	Sep	Oct	Nov	Dec

Grazing	Jan	Feb	Mar	Ap	May	Jun	Jul	Aug	Sep	Oct	Nov	Dec

Medical Record

Illnesses and Injuries History

Date:	Type of Injury or Illness	Treatment

Vaccination & Supplement History Record

Date	Disease	Supplement used	Result

Testing Record History

Date	Test Performed	Results

Parasite Control Record

Date	Method

Kidding & Breeding Record

Bred to: _____   Date: _____

Kid	Name	Sex	Weight	Markings	Tattoo

Bred to: _____   Date: _____

Kid	Name	Sex	Weight	Markings	Tattoo

Bred to: _____   Date: _____

Kid	Name	Sex	Weight	Markings	Tattoo

Goat Information

Name:	Color:	Sire:
Sex:	Breed:	Dame:
Age:	Registration:	ID Number:
Date of birth:	Identifying marks:	

How Acquired: ☐ Purchased ☐ Born in farm ☐ Leased

Keeping purpose: ☐ Sell ☐ Milk ☐ Meat ☐ Pet ☐ Other

Weight Tracker

Birth	Jan	Feb	Mar	AP	Ma	Jun	Jul	Aug	Sep	Oct	Nov	Dec	**Fin**

Feeding Record

Grain	Jan	Feb	Mar	Ap	May	Jun	Jul	Aug	Sep	Oct	Nov	Dec
Grazing	Jan	Feb	Mar	Ap	May	Jun	Jul	Aug	Sep	Oct	Nov	Dec

Medical Record

Illnesses and Injuries History

Date:	Type of Injury or Illness	Treatment

Vaccination & Supplement History Record

Date	Disease	Supplement used	Result

Testing Record History

Date	Test Performed	Results

Parasite Control Record

Date	Method

Kidding & Breeding Record

Bred to: _____   Date: _____

Kid	Name	Sex	Weight	Markings	Tattoo

Bred to: _____   Date: _____

Kid	Name	Sex	Weight	Markings	Tattoo

Bred to: _____   Date: _____

Kid	Name	Sex	Weight	Markings	Tattoo

Goat Information

Name:	Color:	Sire:
Sex:	Breed:	Dame:
Age:	Registration:	ID Number:
Date of birth:	Identifying marks:	

How Acquired: ☐ Purchased ☐ Born in farm ☐ Leased

Keeping purpose: ☐ Sell ☐ Milk ☐ Meat ☐ Pet ☐ Other

Weight Tracker

Birth	Jan	Feb	Mar	AP	Ma	Jun	Jul	Aug	Sep	Oct	Nov	Dec	Fin

Feeding Record

Grain	Jan	Feb	Mar	Ap	May	Jun	Jul	Aug	Sep	Oct	Nov	Dec

Grazing	Jan	Feb	Mar	Ap	May	Jun	Jul	Aug	Sep	Oct	Nov	Dec

Medical Record

Illnesses and Injuries History

Date:	Type of Injury or Illness	Treatment

Vaccination & Supplement History Record

Date	Disease	Supplement used	Result

Testing Record History

Date	Test Performed	Results

Parasite Control Record

Date	Method

Kidding & Breeding Record

Bred to: _____   Date: _____

Kid	Name	Sex	Weight	Markings	Tattoo

Bred to: _____   Date: _____

Kid	Name	Sex	Weight	Markings	Tattoo

Bred to: _____   Date: _____

Kid	Name	Sex	Weight	Markings	Tattoo

Goat Information

Name:	Color:	Sire:
Sex:	Breed:	Dame:
Age:	Registration:	ID Number:
Date of birth:	Identifying marks:	

How Acquired: ☐ Purchased   ☐ Born in farm   ☐ Leased

Keeping purpose: ☐ Sell   ☐ Milk   ☐ Meat   ☐ Pet   ☐ Other

Weight Tracker

Birth	Jan	Feb	Mar	AP	Ma	Jun	Jul	Aug	Sep	Oct	Nov	Dec	Fin

Feeding Record

Grain	Jan	Feb	Mar	Ap	May	Jun	Jul	Aug	Sep	Oct	Nov	Dec
Grazing	Jan	Feb	Mar	Ap	May	Jun	Jul	Aug	Sep	Oct	Nov	Dec

Medical Record

Illnesses and Injuries History

Date:	Type of Injury or Illness	Treatment

Vaccination & Supplement History Record

Date	Disease	Supplement used	Result

Testing Record History

Date	Test Performed	Results

Parasite Control Record

Date	Method

Kidding & Breeding Record

Bred to: _____ Date: _____

Kid	Name	Sex	Weight	Markings	Tattoo

Bred to: _____ Date: _____

Kid	Name	Sex	Weight	Markings	Tattoo

Bred to: _____ Date: _____

Kid	Name	Sex	Weight	Markings	Tattoo

Goat Information

Name:	Color:	Sire:
Sex:	Breed:	Dame:
Age:	Registration:	ID Number:
Date of birth:	Identifying marks:	

How Acquired: ☐ Purchased   ☐ Born in farm   ☐ Leased

Keeping purpose: ☐ Sell   ☐ Milk   ☐ Meat   ☐ Pet   ☐ Other

Weight Tracker

Birth	Jan	Feb	Mar	AP	Ma	Jun	Jul	Aug	Sep	Oct	Nov	Dec	Fin

Feeding Record

Grain	Jan	Feb	Mar	Ap	May	Jun	Jul	Aug	Sep	Oct	Nov	Dec

Grazing	Jan	Feb	Mar	Ap	May	Jun	Jul	Aug	Sep	Oct	Nov	Dec

Medical Record

Illnesses and Injuries History

Date:	Type of Injury or Illness	Treatment

Vaccination & Supplement History Record

Date	Disease	Supplement used	Result

Testing Record History

Date	Test Performed	Results

Parasite Control Record

Date	Method

Kidding & Breeding Record

Bred to: _____ Date: _____

Kid	Name	Sex	Weight	Markings	Tattoo

Bred to: _____ Date: _____

Kid	Name	Sex	Weight	Markings	Tattoo

Bred to: _____ Date: _____

Kid	Name	Sex	Weight	Markings	Tattoo

Notes

Made in the USA
Coppell, TX
12 January 2025

44285087R00063